I0224119

The Deja Vu Enigma:

"Uncovering the Truth About Past Lives and Reincarnation."

Production By:

Branch Zeed Publishing

Edited By: Empress Branch

Branch Zeed Publishing House
Bringing Worlds to Life

Branch Zeed Publishing House

At Branch Zeed Publishing House, we are dedicated to promoting diversity and inclusivity in the books we publish. We believe that all voices deserve to be heard and strive to provide a platform for underrepresented authors and stories. We believe that books have the power to change lives. Whether you're looking for inspiration, entertainment, or education, our selection of books has something for everyone. With a focus on quality, diversity, and accessibility, we're committed to publishing books that make a difference.

Production By: Branch Zeed Publishing House

Edited By: Empress Branch

Printing in the United States

Publishing Co. Summerville, SC 29483

ISBN: 979-8-9877222-3-7

Book production: Branch Zeed Publishing House

branchzeedpublishinghouse@gmail.com

Book Cover: Ahmer Ilyas & Waseem Ilyas

DEDICATION

The author, Ton'te Fairfax, has been experiencing déjà vu since she was a young girl and continues to do so to this day. Determined to understand the mechanics behind this phenomenon, she has dedicated her work to her son **Julius,** her two daughters **Tearia** and **Taleyia**, and her granddaughter **Taniya,** who also occasionally experience déjà vu. Fairfax hopes that this book will be a valuable resource for those seeking a better understanding of déjà vu.

"Bringing worlds to life, one page at a time"

BRANCH ZEED PUBLISHING HOUSE

The Night Hag's Victims

A Deep Dive into the Psychology and
Neuroscience of Sleep Paralysis

Ton'te Fairfax

AVAILABLE NOW

Ton'te Fairfax

Contents

Introduction   09

More Details   11

Chapter 1: Introduction: The Mystery of Deja Vu and Past Lives   13

Chapter 2: A Brief History of Reincarnation: Ancient Beliefs and

    Practices   19

Chapter 3: Scientific Theories and Research on Past Lives and

    Reincarnation   27

Chapter 4: Exploring the Evidence: Case Studies and Personal

    Accounts of Past Life Memories   35

Chapter 5: Accessing Your Own Past Lives: Techniques and

    Exercises for Self-Discovery   39

Chapter 6: Understanding the Role of Past Lives in Your Current Life   43

Chapter 7: The Connection between Past Lives and Karma   47

Chapter 8: The Impact of Past Lives on Relationships and Life Paths   57

Chapter 9: Healing Past Life Trauma and Negative Patterns   77

Chapter 10: The Link between Past Lives and Spiritual Growth

    and Enlightenment   81

Chapter 11: Conclusion: Uncovering the Truth about Past Lives

    and the Deja Vu Enigma.   87

    Suggestions for Further Resources and Support   93

    References   95

    About The Author   97

    Thank You   99

Upcoming Books   100

Introduction

Welcome, dear reader, to "The Deja Vu Enigma: Uncovering the Truth About Past Lives and Reincarnation." This book is a journey of self-discovery and exploration into the mysterious realm of past lives and reincarnation.

For centuries, humanity has been fascinated by the concept of past lives and reincarnation, and the idea that our souls may continue on after death. The phenomenon of deja vu, the feeling of having already experienced a current situation, has long been considered as evidence for past lives.

In this book, we will delve into the history of reincarnation, examining the beliefs and practices of ancient cultures and religions. We will explore the scientific theories and research surrounding past lives and reincarnation, and examine the evidence for and against their existence.

But this book is not just a collection of facts and theories - it is also a guide for you to uncover the truth about your own past lives. Through exercises and meditations, we will explore ways to access your own past life memories and gain a deeper understanding of the role that past lives play in your current life.

As you read, be open to the possibility of past lives and the wisdom they may hold for you. Trust in the journey of your soul, and allow yourself to be guided towards a deeper understanding of the mysteries of existence.

May this book be a shining light on your path towards self-discovery and enlightenment. Namaste.

More Details

Ton'te Fairfax the author of "The Deja Vu Enigma: Uncovering the Truth About Past Lives and Reincarnation" is a thought leader in the field of past lives and reincarnation. Drawing from her personal experiences with deja vu, she delves into the intriguing question of how these occurrences are possible. Throughout the book, she explores the various theories surrounding deja vu and reincarnation, including the possibility of a glitch in the universe or the idea that we may have lived previous lives that we do not remember. With a deep understanding of the subject matter and a unique perspective based on her own experiences, the author presents a compelling case for the existence of past lives and reincarnation. This book is a must-read for anyone interested in understanding the mysteries of the universe and our place in it.

Chapter 1

Introduction: The Mystery of Deja Vu and Past Lives

Deja vu, French for "already seen," is the feeling that one has experienced a current situation before. It is a phenomenon that has puzzled scientists and philosophers for centuries. The experience of deja vu is often accompanied by a strong sense of familiarity and an eerie feeling that the present moment has already occurred in the past.

Past life regression, on the other hand, is a therapeutic technique used to access memories of past lives. The belief behind this technique is that the human soul carries memories of past lives and that these memories can be accessed through hypnosis or other forms of meditation. Proponents of past life regression believe that these memories can help individuals understand and overcome current life issues.

The link between deja vu and past lives is a topic of much debate and speculation. Some experts believe that deja vu is a symptom of past life memories surfacing in the present. Others suggest that deja vu is simply a glitch in the brain's memory system.

There is no scientific evidence to support the idea that past lives exist or that deja vu is caused by past life memories. However, many people continue to be fascinated by the topic and find comfort in the idea that they have lived before. Some experts argue that even if past lives do not exist in a literal sense, the idea of past lives can be used as a tool for self-discovery and personal growth.

The mystery of deja vu and past lives is a topic that continues to intrigue people. While there is no scientific evidence to support the existence of past lives or the link between deja vu and past lives, the idea of past lives can be used as a tool for self-discovery and personal growth. More research is needed to understand the true nature of deja vu and the potential link to past lives.

It's also worth mentioning that some researchers have proposed alternative explanations for the phenomenon of deja vu. For example, some experts suggest that deja vu may be caused by a glitch in the brain's memory system, where the brain mistakenly recognizes a new experience as something that has been encountered before. Others have proposed that deja vu may be the result of a temporary disruption in the brain's ability to distinguish between memories of similar events or places.

Additionally, it's important to note that some people may experience deja vu as a symptom of certain medical conditions or as a side effect of certain medications. Therefore, it's crucial to consult with a medical professional if you experience frequent or severe episodes of deja vu, especially if it is accompanied by other symptoms.

While some people find comfort in the idea of past lives, others may find it unsettling or anxiety-provoking. It's essential for individuals to approach the topic with an open mind and respect for their personal beliefs and feelings.

The topic of deja vu and past lives is a complex and multifaceted one that continues to intrigue and fascinate many people. There is currently no scientific evidence to support the existence of past lives or the link between deja vu and past lives. However, the idea of past lives can be used as a tool for self-discovery and personal growth.

Some researchers have studied the psychological and emotional benefits of exploring past life memories and the idea of reincarnation. For example, some experts argue that exploring past life memories can help individuals to gain insight into their current life struggles and emotions, and help them to understand and process unresolved issues. Additionally, some therapists argue that past life regression therapy can help individuals to identify and release unconscious patterns and behaviors that may be holding them back in their current life.

However, it's important to note that these benefits are not scientifically proven, and the majority of experts in the field consider that the idea of past lives is not a scientifically validated concept. Therefore, it's important for individuals to approach the topic with an open mind and respect for different perspectives.

In summary, the idea of past lives and reincarnation remains a topic of ongoing debate and research. While there is currently no scientific evidence to support the existence of past lives or the link between deja vu and past lives, many people continue to find comfort and meaning in the idea. The psychological and emotional benefits of exploring past lives have not been scientifically proven and it is important to approach the topic with an open mind, respect for different perspectives.

The idea of past lives can be used as a tool for self-discovery and personal growth, regardless of whether or not it is a scientifically proven concept. For example, exploring the idea of past lives can help individuals to gain a different perspective on their current life experiences, and can also provide a sense of connection and continuity with the past. It can also provide a sense of purpose and meaning for some individuals.

It's also worth noting that even if past lives do not exist in a literal sense, the concept of reincarnation can be used as a metaphor for understanding the human experience. For example, it can be used to explore the idea of cyclical patterns in life, or to consider the idea that we are constantly evolving and growing as individuals.

It's also important to remember that the belief in reincarnation is a personal decision and should be respected as such. It's ultimately up to each individual to decide what they believe about past lives and reincarnation, and how they want to integrate the concept into their personal beliefs and practices.

It is also important to mention that while the scientific community has not found any concrete evidence to support the existence of past lives or reincarnation, there are still many people who claim to have memories of past lives, and some of these memories can be quite detailed and vivid. Many people find these memories to be meaningful and validating, even if they cannot be scientifically verified.

Additionally, it's worth mentioning that belief in past lives and reincarnation is not limited to certain cultures or religions, it can be found in many different cultures and traditions throughout history. This suggests that the idea of past lives and reincarnation may be a universal concept that has resonated with people across time and cultures.

Furthermore, the concept of past lives and reincarnation has been explored in literature, art, and popular culture. From ancient texts to modern movies and books, the theme of past lives and reincarnation continues to capture the imagination of people. This further highlights the fact that the idea of past lives and reincarnation continues to be an important and intriguing concept for many people.

The topic of past lives and reincarnation continues to be a subject of ongoing debate and research, with many people finding comfort and meaning in the idea of past lives, even if it cannot be scientifically proven. The concept of past lives and reincarnation has been an important aspect of many cultures and religions throughout history and continues to be held by many people today. It's important to approach the topic with an open mind and respect for different perspectives.

It's also worth mentioning that some people may find the idea of past lives and reincarnation to be a source of inspiration and motivation. For example, the idea that we have lived before and will live again can be a reminder to live life to the fullest and make the most of the time we have. It can also serve as a reminder to be kind and compassionate towards others, as we may have been connected to them in previous lives.

The concept of past lives and reincarnation can also be used as a tool for self-reflection and introspection. For example, exploring past life memories or the idea of reincarnation can help individuals to gain insight into their own personal history, beliefs and patterns. It can also serve as a reminder that we are all interconnected and that our actions have consequences. Many people find comfort in the idea that our loved ones who have passed away may still be with us in some form, and that we will see them again in future lives. This can provide a sense of closure and peace for those who have lost loved ones.

The Deja Vu Enigma

"Uncovering the Truth About Past Lives and Reincarnation."

<u>Chapter 2</u>

A Brief History of Reincarnation: Ancient Beliefs and Practices

Reincarnation is the belief that the soul or spirit of a living being continues to exist after death and is reborn in a new body. This belief has been held by various cultures and religions throughout history, and has been an important aspect of many ancient belief systems.

In ancient Egyptian religion, for example, the concept of reincarnation was closely tied to the idea of an afterlife. The Egyptians believed that the soul of a deceased person would travel to the underworld, where it would be judged by the god Osiris. If the soul was found to be pure, it would be granted eternal life in the afterlife. This concept is reflected in the practice of mummification, which was intended to preserve the body so that the soul could return to it in the afterlife.

In ancient Greece, the idea of reincarnation was also present in various religious and philosophical traditions. The Pythagoreans, a group of philosophers who were active in the 6th century BCE, believed that the soul was immortal and that it could be reincarnated in different forms. The Orphics, a religious sect that emerged in the 6th century BCE, also believed in reincarnation and held that the soul was punished or rewarded in the afterlife depending on the actions of the previous life.

In ancient India, the belief in reincarnation was central to the religious and philosophical traditions of Hinduism, Jainism, and Buddhism. In Hinduism, the belief in reincarnation is closely tied to the concept of karma, which holds that the actions of an individual in one life will determine their fate in future lives. In Jainism, the belief in reincarnation is closely tied to the concept of non-violence and the desire to free the soul from the cycle of birth and death. Buddhism, which originated in India in the 6th century BCE, also teaches the belief in reincarnation and the concept of karma, and holds that the ultimate goal of the individual is to achieve enlightenment and escape the cycle of birth and death.

In ancient China, the belief in reincarnation was present in various religious and philosophical traditions. The concept of reincarnation is seen in the religious traditions of Taoism, which holds that the soul of the deceased can be reincarnated in a new body.

The Deja Vu Enigma

Overall, the belief in reincarnation has been an important aspect of many ancient belief systems throughout history. It has been present in the religious and philosophical traditions of ancient Egypt, Greece, India, China, and many other cultures. The concept of reincarnation continues to be held by many people today and is an important aspect of certain modern religions and spiritual practices.

In addition to the ancient cultures and religions previously mentioned, the belief in reincarnation has also been present in many other cultures and religions throughout history. In ancient Persia, for example, the Zoroastrian religion believed in the concept of the "Fravashi," which is a person's spiritual essence that continues to exist after death and can be reincarnated in a new body. In ancient Mesopotamia, the religion of the Assyrians and Babylonians included the belief in the "Ekur," a type of afterlife where the soul of the deceased could be reincarnated.

In many indigenous cultures, the belief in reincarnation is closely tied to the concept of the "spirit world," where the spirits of the deceased can continue to exist and potentially be reincarnated. This is the case in many Native American cultures, where the belief in reincarnation is closely tied to the concept of the "ghost dance," a spiritual practice intended to bring the spirits of the deceased back to life.

In many African cultures, the belief in reincarnation is closely tied to the concept of ancestor worship. Ancestor worship is the belief that the spirits of deceased ancestors can continue to exist and potentially be reincarnated, and is closely tied to the concept of the "ancestral realm," where the spirits of the deceased can continue to exist.

In modern times, the belief in reincarnation is still held by many people, particularly in certain religious and spiritual practices. In certain strains of the New Age movement, the belief in reincarnation is closely tied to the concept of "past lives," where individuals can access memories of previous lives through techniques such as past life regression. In certain sects of Hinduism, Buddhism and Jainism, the belief in reincarnation is also an important aspect of their spiritual practice.

Overall, the belief in reincarnation has been an important aspect of many cultures and religions throughout history and continues to be held by many people today. It is a complex and multifaceted concept that can be understood and interpreted in many different ways, depending on the culture or religion in which it is found.

Additionally, in certain spiritual and religious practices, the belief in reincarnation is closely tied to the concept of karma. Karma refers to the principle that actions and choices in one's current life will determine the nature of one's future lives. This belief holds that individuals are responsible for their own actions and that the consequences of these actions will be experienced in future lives. This concept is central to many Eastern religions such as Hinduism, Buddhism, and Jainism.

In some New Age and alternative spiritual practices, the belief in reincarnation is often tied to the idea of spiritual evolution and personal growth. This belief holds that the soul incarnates in different physical bodies over time in order to learn and grow, and that each lifetime offers new opportunities for spiritual growth and development.

Overall, the belief in reincarnation is a complex and multifaceted concept that can be understood and interpreted in many different ways. It's an important aspect of many cultures and religions throughout history and continues to be held by many people today. It's important to respect and acknowledge the diversity of beliefs and perspectives when exploring this topic.

Furthermore, it's worth noting that the belief in reincarnation is not limited to ancient or Eastern cultures and religions, it can also be found in some Western spiritual and religious traditions such as certain sects of Christianity, Gnosticism, and Kabbalah. These beliefs often have a different interpretation of the concept, such as reincarnation being seen as a process of spiritual development and purification rather than a physical rebirth.

Moreover, the belief in reincarnation is also found in some forms of contemporary spirituality, such as some forms of neo-paganism, Wicca and certain forms of New Age spirituality. These spiritual practices often focus on the idea of a cyclical and interconnected universe, where the soul is seen as eternal and constantly evolving.

It's also important to note that belief in reincarnation is not limited to religion or spirituality, but can also be found in some philosophical and metaphysical theories. Some philosophers and metaphysicians argue that the concept of reincarnation can offer a way to understand the nature of existence and the relationship between the individual self and the greater universe.

The belief in reincarnation is a complex and multifaceted concept that has been an important aspect of many cultures and religions throughout history and continues to be held by many people today. It is diversely interpreted and understood, and can be found in many different spiritual, religious, philosophical and metaphysical traditions.

It's also worth noting that the concept of reincarnation is not without its critics and skeptics. Many people argue that the belief in reincarnation is based on faith rather than evidence, and that there is currently no scientific evidence to support the existence of past lives or reincarnation. Critics also argue that the belief in reincarnation can be used to justify social and economic inequalities, by suggesting that people's station in life is a result of their actions in past lives.

Moreover, some argue that belief in reincarnation can also create a sense of fatalism and apathy, as people may believe that their current circumstances are predetermined by their actions in past lives and that they cannot change their current reality.

Additionally, some argue that belief in reincarnation may not be psychologically healthy, as it can create feelings of guilt, anxiety and fear about past lives and future lives.

However, it's important to remember that the belief in reincarnation is a personal decision and should be respected as such. It's also important to note that, regardless of one's belief in reincarnation, it's important to live in the present, take responsibility for our actions and strive to make the world a better place for ourselves and for others.

Belief in reincarnation is a complex and multifaceted concept with a diverse range of beliefs and interpretations. It's important to approach the topic with an open mind and respect for different perspectives, and to remember that it remains a subject of personal belief and faith.

The Deja Vu Enigma

"Uncovering the Truth About Past Lives and Reincarnation."

Chapter 3

Scientific Theories and Research on Past Lives and Reincarnation

The concept of past lives and reincarnation is a complex and controversial topic that has been studied by many scientists and researchers in various fields of study. However, despite a significant amount of research, there is currently no scientific evidence that definitively proves the existence of past lives or reincarnation.

One of the main theories in the scientific study of past lives and reincarnation is the concept of past life regression. This theory suggests that memories of past lives can be accessed through hypnosis or other forms of therapy, and that these memories can provide insight into the individual's current life and issues they may be facing. However, many scientists and researchers have criticized this theory, as there is little scientific evidence to support the validity of these memories and the methods used to access them. Furthermore, many experts argue that the memories accessed during past life regression may be nothing more than the product of the individual's imagination, or a result of suggestion from the therapist.

Another theory related to past lives and reincarnation is the concept of genetic memory. This theory suggests that memories and traits of past lives can be passed down through genetic material and manifest in an individual's current life. However, there is currently no scientific evidence that supports this theory, and most experts in the field consider it to be highly speculative.

Overall, while the idea of past lives and reincarnation is an intriguing and fascinating topic, there is currently no scientific evidence that definitively proves its existence. Many theories and hypotheses have been proposed, but they all remain unproven, and the majority of experts in the field are skeptical of their validity.

Additionally, there are also cultural, religious and philosophical perspectives on reincarnation. Many ancient cultures have belief in reincarnation as a core part of their religious or spiritual practices. It is often seen as a way to explain the continued existence of the soul after death, or to provide a framework for understanding the cycles of life and death. However, it is important to note that these beliefs are not based on scientific evidence and are often rooted in tradition and faith.

The Deja Vu Enigma

In Philosophy, reincarnation has been discussed as a way to explain the problem of personal identity. The concept of rebirth allows for the continuity of personal identity over time, despite the fact that the body and mind change.

While there is currently no scientific evidence that definitively proves the existence of past lives or reincarnation, the topic remains a subject of ongoing debate and research. It is important to consider both scientific and non-scientific perspectives when exploring this topic.

It's also worth mentioning that some scientists and researchers have proposed alternative explanations for the phenomenon of past life memories. For example, some have suggested that these memories may be the result of cryptomnesia, which is the unconscious recollection of previously learned information that is not currently in conscious awareness. Others have proposed that past life memories may be the result of epigenetics, which is the study of how environmental factors can affect gene expression.

Despite the lack of scientific evidence, many people continue to claim that they have memories of past lives, and some even claim to have vivid, detailed memories of specific historical events. These claims have led some researchers to study the phenomenon of past life memories in more depth, in an attempt to understand the underlying mechanisms and factors that may be involved.

It's important to consider that past lives and reincarnation are not an accepted scientific theory, and there is no scientific consensus on the matter. Belief in past lives and reincarnation is based on personal belief and faith, and it is not proven or disproven by science.

It's also worth noting that some researchers have sought to study past lives and reincarnation using methods such as case studies, interviews, and surveys. These methods aim to gather information about people's past life memories and experiences, in an attempt to understand the nature and characteristics of these memories. However, it's important to note that these methods are not considered scientifically rigorous, and the results of such studies are often considered to be anecdotal and open to interpretation.

Moreover, there have been some studies which suggest that past life memories may be the result of psychological factors, such as childhood experiences, or unresolved emotional issues. These theories suggest that past life memories may be a manifestation of the mind's attempt to make sense of present-day experiences and emotions, rather than a literal recollection of past lives.

Overall, the scientific study of past lives and reincarnation remains a complex and controversial topic. While many theories and hypotheses have been proposed, there is currently no scientific evidence that definitively proves the existence of past lives or reincarnation. The majority of scientists and researchers are skeptical of the validity of past life memories and the methods used to access them, and consider that it remains a subject of personal belief and faith.

It's also worth mentioning that there are some who argue that the lack of scientific evidence for past lives and reincarnation does not necessarily mean that it does not exist. They argue that the concept of past lives and reincarnation may be beyond the current capabilities of science to measure or prove. They suggest that, just as science has not yet been able to prove the existence of other phenomena such as dark matter or consciousness, it may never be able to prove the existence of past lives and reincarnation.

Additionally, some argue that the study of past lives and reincarnation is not limited to scientific study, but can also be explored through spiritual and contemplative practices such as meditation, self-reflection, and spiritual guidance. These practices aim to gain insight and understanding of the nature of existence, and the relationship between the individual self and the greater universe.

In summary, while the scientific study of past lives and reincarnation remains inconclusive, the topic continues to be of interest to many people. The lack of scientific evidence does not necessarily mean that it doesn't exist, and it may be explored through other means such as personal reflection, spiritual practices, and philosophical inquiry. Ultimately, the belief or nonbelief in past lives and reincarnation is a personal decision and should be respected as such.

It's also worth mentioning that some researchers have looked into the potential benefits of past life regression therapy. While there is no scientific evidence that supports the validity of past life memories accessed through such therapy, some argue that the process can have therapeutic benefits. For example, it can help individuals gain insight into their current life struggles and emotions, and help them to understand and process unresolved issues. Additionally, some therapists argue that past life regression therapy can help individuals to identify and release unconscious patterns and behaviors that may be holding them back in their current life.

However, it's important to note that past life regression therapy is not a scientifically validated form of therapy, and it's not recognized by mainstream psychological or psychiatric organizations. Furthermore, it's crucial to seek out a qualified and trained professional when considering past life regression therapy, as there are many unqualified practitioners who may not have the necessary skills and training to provide safe and effective therapy.

While the scientific study of past lives and reincarnation is ongoing and inconclusive, the concept of past lives and reincarnation remains a topic of interest and debate. The potential therapeutic benefits of past life regression therapy is not scientifically proven, but some practitioners and individuals argue that it can be beneficial. It's important to approach the topic with an open mind and respect for different perspectives, and to seek out qualified professional help if considering past life regression therapy.

It's also worth mentioning that some researchers have looked into the phenomenon of children who claim to have memories of past lives, known as "past life memories in children" or "reincarnation in children" phenomenon. Some researchers believe that these children's claims may be more credible than those of adults, as they have not yet been exposed to cultural or societal influences that may shape their beliefs about past lives and reincarnation. Some studies have been conducted on these children's claims, but it's important to note that these studies are not considered scientifically rigorous, and the results are often considered to be anecdotal and open to interpretation.

However, it's important to note that the majority of scientists and researchers in the field of psychology and psychiatry consider that these claims are highly unlikely to be true past life memories, and are more likely to be the result of the child's imagination or the influence of adults.

Additionally, it's important to consider the psychological and emotional well-being of the child when dealing with these claims. The idea of a past life can be confusing and overwhelming for a child, and it's important to approach the topic with sensitivity and caution.

While the concept of past lives and reincarnation remains a topic of ongoing debate and research, the phenomenon of past life memories in children is not widely accepted by the scientific community. There is currently no scientific evidence that supports the validity of these claims, and it's important to approach the topic with caution and sensitivity.

Another aspect worth mentioning is the fact that some people have reported having spontaneous past life memories, or memories that appear without the use of hypnosis or any other form of therapy. These memories can take the form of vivid flashbacks, dreams, or even physical sensations that seem to be associated with a past life. While some researchers have studied this phenomenon, it's important to note that there is currently no scientific evidence to support the validity of these memories, and it's generally considered to be a rare occurrence.

Additionally, it's important to note that many people who claim to have past life memories may have other underlying psychological or emotional issues that are causing them to have these experiences. For example, some people may have unresolved trauma or other emotional issues that are manifesting as past life memories.

In any case, it's important to approach the topic of past lives and reincarnation with an open mind and a healthy dose of skepticism. While the concept is intriguing and fascinating, it's important to remember that there is currently no scientific evidence to support the validity of past life memories, and that the majority of experts in the field are skeptical of their validity. It is always recommended to consult with a qualified professional if you have any concerns about your mental health or emotional well-being.

The Deja Vu Enigma

"Uncovering the Truth About Past Lives and Reincarnation."

Chapter 4

Exploring the Evidence: Case Studies and Personal Accounts of Past Life Memories

Past life memories, also known as reincarnation or rebirth, is the belief that the soul or consciousness of a person continues to exist after death and is reborn in a new body. While the concept of reincarnation is a central tenet in some religions, such as Hinduism and Buddhism, it is not a widely accepted idea in Western culture. However, there have been many case studies and personal accounts of past life memories that have been documented over the years.

One of the most well-known cases of past life memories is that of Bridey Murphy. In the 1950s, a woman named Virginia Tighe underwent hypnosis and claimed to have vivid memories of a past life as an Irish woman named Bridey Murphy. She provided specific details about the life of Bridey Murphy, including her name, her family members, and the location of her home. While some skeptics dismissed these memories as the result of suggestion or imagination, others believed that they were genuine past life memories.

Another famous case of past life memories is that of James Leininger, a young boy who began having nightmares about being in a plane crash at a very young age. He would wake up screaming, "Airplane crash! Plane on fire! Little man can't get out!" His parents were puzzled and consulted with a therapist. As the boy grew older, he began to provide more detailed information about the plane crash and his past life as a pilot in World War II.

In addition to these case studies, there have been numerous personal accounts of past life memories from individuals who have experienced flashbacks, vivid dreams, or a sense of déjà vu. Some people claim to have memories of specific historical events or famous figures, while others claim to have memories of more mundane aspects of past lives.

While there is no scientific evidence to support the idea of reincarnation, many people find comfort and meaning in the idea that their consciousness may continue to exist after death. However, it's important to note that many of these case studies and personal accounts are based on anecdotal evidence and are therefore difficult to verify. Additionally, scientific research on past life memories has been hampered by the lack of a consistent methodology and the difficulty of verifying the accuracy of the memories.

The Deja Vu Enigma

While the concept of past life memories and reincarnation is not widely accepted in Western culture, there have been many case studies and personal accounts of past life memories that have been documented over the years. The accuracy of these memories and the validity of the concept of reincarnation remains a topic of debate among experts in the field.

The Deja Vu Enigma

"Uncovering the Truth About Past Lives and
Reincarnation."

Chapter 5

Accessing Your Own Past Lives: Techniques and Exercises for Self-Discovery

Accessing past lives is a technique used to explore and gain insight into one's past lives, which are believed to be stored in the subconscious mind. This practice can be used for self-discovery and personal growth, as well as to understand the origins of certain patterns or behaviors in one's current life.

There are several techniques and exercises that can be used to access past lives, including:

1.   Past Life Regression: This technique involves going into a deep state of relaxation through hypnosis, guided imagery, or meditation, and then accessing memories of past lives. A trained therapist or guide can assist in this process, helping the individual to explore and understand their past lives.

2.   Active Imagination: This technique involves using the imagination to actively create a scene from a past life and then observing and interacting with the characters and events in that scene. This can be done through writing, drawing, or other forms of self-expression.

3.   Journaling: Writing about past life memories or experiences can be a powerful tool for accessing and understanding them. Keeping a journal of these experiences can also help to identify patterns and connections between past lives and current experiences.

4.   Meditation: Meditation can help to quiet the mind and access deeper levels of consciousness, where past life memories may be stored. Guided meditations specifically tailored to past life regression can be helpful.

5.   Dream work: Dreams can be a powerful tool for accessing past life memories. Keeping a dream journal and reflecting on recurrent dreams, symbols, and themes can help to uncover past life experiences.

It's important to note that accessing past lives is a subjective experience and the validity of past life memories can't be confirmed or denied by science. It's also worth mentioning that not everyone believes in the concept of past lives, and that these techniques and exercises are intended for individuals who are open to the possibility of past lives as a tool for self-discovery.

It's important to approach the exploration of past lives with an open mind and a willingness to suspend judgment. It's also recommended to work with a therapist or guide who is trained and experienced in working with past lives, to help to navigate the process in a safe and supportive way.

Another technique for accessing past lives is called "age regression" or "age progression" which is a form of hypnotherapy. During this process, the individual is taken back in time to a specific age or period in their current life, and then guided to explore memories, emotions, and events from that time. This can be used to uncover repressed memories or traumas that may be impacting the individual's current life.

Another technique is called "past life visualization", where the individual uses visualization and creative imagination to see themselves in different past lives. This can be done through guided visualization or through self-directed visualization. This technique is often used to explore different scenarios or possibilities of past lives, and can be a powerful tool for self-discovery and personal growth.

It is important to note that some people may have a hard time accessing past lives memories, and that's okay. It's important to remember that the goal of these techniques is self-discovery, not to prove or disprove the existence of past lives. The most important thing is to approach the process with an open mind and a willingness to explore.

Some people may have past life memories that are traumatic, and it is important to approach these memories with care and caution. It's recommended to work with a therapist or guide who is trained in dealing with traumatic memories to help process and integrate these experiences in a safe and healthy way.

Additionally, it's important to remember that these are self-discovery techniques and not intended as a replacement for professional medical or psychological treatment. It's important to seek professional help if you have any concerns about your mental or physical health.

In conclusion, accessing past lives can be a powerful tool for self-discovery and personal growth. There are various techniques and exercises that can be used to explore past lives, including past life regression, active imagination, journaling, meditation, dream work, age regression, and past life visualization. It's important to approach the exploration of past lives with an open mind and to work with a trained therapist or guide to navigate the process in a safe and supportive way.

Chapter 6

Understanding the Role of Past Lives in Your Current Life

The concept of past lives refers to the belief that individuals have lived previous lives, and that the experiences and events from these past lives can influence and shape one's current life. This belief is held by some Eastern religions, such as Hinduism and Buddhism, as well as by some New Age spiritual practices.

One way past lives are believed to impact the current life is through the concept of karma. Karma refers to the belief that one's actions in past lives determine their current circumstances and experiences. Good actions lead to positive karma and future happiness, while negative actions lead to negative karma and future suffering.

Another way past lives are believed to influence the current life is through the concept of reincarnation. Reincarnation refers to the belief that after death, the soul is reborn in a new body and continues on its journey of spiritual growth. The experiences and lessons from past lives are believed to carry over into the current life and shape one's personality, talents, and challenges.

Some people believe that past life memories can be accessed through techniques such as hypnosis or meditation. This is often referred to as past life regression, and it is believed that by exploring past lives, individuals can gain insight into their current life issues and make positive changes.

It's important to note that past life belief is a matter of personal belief and faith and there is no scientific evidence to support the existence of past lives. Some people may find comfort and guidance in exploring past lives, while others may not find it relevant to their life or spiritual beliefs.

The concept of past lives holds that individuals have lived previous lives and that the experiences and events from these past lives can influence and shape one's current life through the concepts of karma and reincarnation. The belief and understanding of past lives varies from person to person and there is no scientific evidence to support it. It's a matter of personal belief and faith.

Another way that past lives can influence the current life is through the concept of unfinished business. According to this belief, unresolved issues or unfinished tasks from a past life can carry over into the current life, manifesting as recurring patterns, unresolved emotions, or unfulfilled desires. By identifying and resolving these issues, individuals can break free from these patterns and find a sense of peace and fulfillment in their current life.

Past life beliefs can also provide explanations for certain aspects of one's current life, such as unexplained phobias or aversions, or a sense of familiarity with certain people or places. Some people believe that these experiences can be linked to past lives. For example, an individual may have a phobia of heights and believe that this fear is rooted in a past life where they were harmed or killed in a fall.

On the other hand, it's important to note that past life memories can be influenced by imagination, fantasy or suggestion during hypnosis, it's important for a therapist or practitioner to approach the subject with caution, and to consider the possibility of confabulation, which means that the person is creating a story that is not true but seems real to them.

Overall, the concept of past lives can be a complex and nuanced topic, and different people may have different beliefs and understandings of how past lives impact the current life. Some people may find comfort and guidance in exploring past lives, while others may not find it relevant to their life or spiritual beliefs. It's important for individuals to approach the subject with an open mind and to consider their own personal beliefs and experiences.

Additionally, it's important to note that the concept of past lives is not a widely accepted or scientifically proven theory. While some people may find comfort and guidance in exploring past lives, there is currently no scientific evidence to support the existence of past lives or the impact that they may have on the current life.

Furthermore, it's worth noting that the idea of past lives can be used to explain away personal responsibility, and can be used as an excuse for not taking action to change one's current life. While exploring past lives can be an interesting and enlightening experience, it's important for individuals to keep in mind that ultimately, it's their actions in the present that shape their future.

Additionally, it's important to remember that past life beliefs and experiences can be highly personal and emotional. It's important to approach the subject with sensitivity and respect, and to remember that what may be true for one person may not be true for another. Each individual's past life beliefs and experiences should be considered on a case by case basis.

This topic can evoke different reactions and reactions. It's important to approach the subject with an open mind and to consider one's own personal beliefs and experiences. It's also important to remember that past life beliefs and experiences are not widely accepted or scientifically proven, and it's important to keep in mind that ultimately, it's one's actions in the present that shape their future.

The Deja Vu Enigma

"Uncovering the Truth About Past Lives and Reincarnation."

Chapter 7

The Connection between Past Lives and Karma

The connection between past lives and karma is a complex and nuanced topic that is rooted in ancient spiritual beliefs and practices. Karma is a central concept in many Eastern religions, including Hinduism, Buddhism, and Jainism, and it refers to the idea that one's actions in this life will have consequences in future lives. According to this belief, good actions will lead to positive outcomes, while negative actions will lead to negative consequences.

In many Eastern spiritual traditions, the concept of past lives is closely tied to the idea of karma. According to these beliefs, the actions and experiences of one's past lives can influence the present and future lives through the accumulation of karma. The idea is that the karma from past lives can manifest in the form of physical, emotional, and mental patterns, experiences, and circumstances in the current life.

For example, an individual who has accumulated negative karma from past lives may experience negative patterns, such as chronic health issues or financial difficulties in their current life. On the other hand, an individual who has accumulated positive karma may experience positive patterns, such as good health and financial prosperity.

Some spiritual practitioners believe that by understanding the connections between past lives and karma, they can gain insight into the patterns and experiences of their current life, and make conscious choices to change negative patterns and experiences. They believe that by resolving the unresolved issues of the past lives, one can break free from negative patterns and experiences and achieve a sense of peace and fulfillment in the present.

It's worth noting that the connection between past lives and karma is not a widely accepted or scientifically proven theory. While some people may find comfort and guidance in exploring the connections between past lives and karma, it's important to remember that there is currently no scientific evidence to support the existence of past lives or the impact that they may have on the current life.

Additionally, it's important to approach the subject of past lives and karma with caution, as the memories can be influenced by imagination, fantasy or suggestion during hypnosis and it's important for a therapist or practitioner to consider the possibility of confabulation, which means that the person is creating a story that is not true but seems real to them.

The connection between past lives and karma is a complex and nuanced topic that is rooted in ancient spiritual beliefs and practices. It's important to approach the subject with an open mind and to consider one's own personal beliefs and experiences. However, it's also important to remember that the connection between past lives and karma is not widely accepted or scientifically proven, and it's important to keep in mind that ultimately, it's one's actions in the present that shape their future.

Another aspect of the connection between past lives and karma is the idea of reincarnation. According to this belief, the soul or consciousness of an individual is reborn into a new body after death. This allows the individual to continue their journey of spiritual growth and development, and to work through any unresolved issues or karma from past lives.

The concept of reincarnation also suggests that people may have lived multiple lives, and that their current life is just one of many. This belief can provide a sense of continuity and purpose to an individual's life, and can help them understand the connections between their current experiences and their past lives.

In some spiritual traditions, the concept of past lives and karma is closely tied to the idea of spiritual evolution and the attainment of enlightenment.

According to these beliefs, the soul is on a journey of spiritual growth and development, and the experiences of past lives and the accumulation of karma are all part of this journey.

The idea is that by understanding and resolving the unresolved issues and karma from past lives, an individual can progress along their spiritual journey and ultimately reach a state of enlightenment.

It's important to note that the concept of past lives and karma is not universally accepted and different people may have different beliefs and understandings of how past lives impact the current life. Some people may find comfort and guidance in exploring past lives, while others may not find it relevant to their life or spiritual beliefs.

It's also important to remember that the concept of past lives and karma is not universally accepted and it is not a widely accepted or scientifically proven theory. It's important to approach the subject with an open mind and to consider one's own personal beliefs and experiences. It's also important to keep in mind that ultimately, it's one's actions in the present that shape their future.

The connection between past lives and karma is a complex and nuanced topic that is rooted in ancient spiritual beliefs and practices. It can provide a sense of continuity and purpose to an individual's life, and can help them understand the connections between their current experiences and their past lives. While some people may find comfort and guidance in exploring past lives, it's important to remember that the connection between past lives and karma is not universally accepted and not scientifically proven. It's important for individuals to approach the subject with an open mind and to consider their own personal beliefs and experiences.

Additionally, it's worth mentioning that the concept of past lives and karma can also be applied to understanding and resolving relationship issues. Some people believe that the unresolved issues and karma from past lives can manifest in the form of relationship patterns, such as attraction to certain types of people, or difficulty in maintaining healthy relationships. According to this belief, by understanding and resolving the unresolved issues and karma from past lives, an individual can break free from negative relationship patterns and attract healthier and more fulfilling relationships in the present.

Furthermore, the concept of past lives and karma can also be applied to understanding and resolving career and professional issues. Some people believe that unresolved issues and karma from past lives can manifest in the form of career and professional patterns, such as difficulty in achieving success or feeling unfulfilled in one's work. According to this belief, by understanding and resolving the unresolved issues and karma from past lives, an individual can break free from negative career and professional patterns and achieve greater success and fulfillment in their current profession.

It's also important to note that the concept of past lives and karma can be used in a therapeutic context. Some therapists and practitioners use past life regression therapy to help individuals explore and understand their past lives and the unresolved issues and karma that may be impacting their current life. However, it's important to approach these therapies with caution, as there is currently no scientific evidence to support their effectiveness and it's important for a therapist or practitioner to consider the possibility of confabulation, which means that the person is creating a story that is not true but seems real to them.

The connection between past lives and karma is a complex and nuanced topic that can be applied to understanding and resolving a wide range of issues, including physical, emotional, and mental patterns, relationship issues, career and professional issues. While some people may find comfort and guidance in exploring past lives and karma, it's important to remember that the connection between past lives and karma is not universally accepted and not scientifically proven. It's important for individuals to approach the subject with an open mind and to consider their own personal beliefs and experiences. And it's important for individuals to be cautious when engaging in past life regression therapy.

It's also important to consider the cultural context when discussing the connection between past lives and karma. In many Eastern cultures, the belief in past lives and karma is deeply ingrained in the cultural and spiritual practices. It is considered a fundamental concept that shapes the way individuals understand themselves and the world around them. In these cultures, the belief in past lives and karma is often intertwined with other spiritual concepts, such as the idea of spiritual evolution and the attainment of enlightenment.

On the other hand, in Western cultures, the belief in past lives and karma is not as widely accepted and is often considered a more alternative or fringe belief. However, in recent years, there has been a growing interest in Eastern spiritual practices and beliefs, including the concept of past lives and karma. This has led to an increasing number of Westerners exploring and incorporating these concepts into their personal beliefs and practices.

It's also important to note that the concept of past lives and karma can be a personal and emotional topic. It's essential to approach the subject with sensitivity and respect, and to remember that what may be true for one person may not be true for another. Each individual's past life beliefs and experiences should be considered on a case by case basis.

Additionally, it's crucial to remember that the connection between past lives and karma is not a universally accepted or scientifically proven theory. It's important to approach the subject with an open mind and to consider one's own personal beliefs and experiences, but also to be cautious about accepting it as a fact without any scientific evidence.

The connection between past lives and karma is a complex and nuanced topic that is rooted in ancient spiritual beliefs and practices. It's important to approach the subject with an open mind and to consider one's own personal beliefs and experiences, but also to be cautious about accepting it as a fact without any scientific evidence. It's also important to consider the cultural context and to approach the subject with sensitivity and respect, and to remember that what may be true for one person may not be true for another.

It's also worth mentioning that the connection between past lives and karma can be a powerful tool for personal growth and self-discovery. By exploring past lives and understanding the unresolved issues and karma that may be impacting their current life, individuals can gain insight into their own behavior patterns, emotions, and experiences. This can help them identify and overcome limiting beliefs, negative patterns, and unresolved issues, leading to greater self-awareness, personal growth, and inner peace.

Additionally, the concept of past lives and karma can provide a sense of meaning and purpose to an individual's life. By understanding the connections between their current experiences and their past lives, individuals can gain a deeper understanding of their personal journey and the role they play in the larger cosmic scheme. This can provide them with a sense of direction and purpose, and can help them navigate the challenges and opportunities of their current life.

There are different methods and techniques that can be used to explore past lives and understand the connection between past lives and karma. Some people may choose to use meditation, journaling, or visualization to access their past lives, while others may prefer to work with a trained therapist or practitioner who specializes in past life regression therapy. It's important to find a method or technique that resonates with one's personal beliefs and experiences.

This belief is rooted in ancient spiritual beliefs and practices. It can provide a sense of continuity, purpose and meaning to an individual's life, and can help them understand the connections between their current experiences and their past lives. By exploring past lives and understanding the unresolved issues and karma that may be impacting their current life, individuals can gain insight into their own behavior patterns, emotions, and experiences. However, it's important to remember that the connection between past lives and karma is not universally accepted and not scientifically proven. It's important to approach the subject with an open mind and to consider one's own personal beliefs and experiences, but also to be cautious about accepting it as a fact without any scientific evidence.

Ton'te Fairfax

Chapter 8

The Impact of Past Lives on Relationships and Life Paths

The impact of past lives on relationships and life paths is a complex and nuanced topic that is rooted in the belief that unresolved issues and experiences from past lives can carry over and influence current relationships and life paths. According to this belief, past lives can shape an individual's behavior patterns, emotions, and experiences in their current life, which can impact their relationships and life paths.

One way that past lives can impact relationships is through the concept of soulmates or twin flames. Some people believe that certain individuals are connected through past lives and that they are meant to meet and be in a relationship in this life. These relationships can be incredibly powerful and fulfilling, but they can also be challenging and difficult, as past life issues and karma can surface and create tension in the relationship.

Another way that past lives can impact relationships is through the concept of unfinished business. According to this belief, unresolved issues or unfinished tasks from a past life can carry over into the current life, manifesting as recurring patterns, unresolved emotions, or unfulfilled desires. These unresolved issues can create tension and conflict in relationships, as individuals may struggle to understand and resolve the underlying issues.

Past lives can also impact life paths by influencing an individual's career and professional choices. Some people believe that unresolved issues or experiences from past lives can manifest as blocks or obstacles in an individual's career and professional life. By understanding and resolving these issues, individuals can break free from negative patterns and achieve greater success and fulfillment in their current profession.

The concept of past lives can also provide explanations for certain aspects of one's current life, such as unexplained phobias or aversions, or a sense of familiarity with certain people or places. Some people believe that these experiences can be linked to past lives. For example, an individual may have a phobia of heights and believe that this fear is rooted in a past life where they were harmed or killed in a fall.

It's important to note that the belief in past lives and the impact on current relationships and life paths is not universally accepted and not scientifically proven. While some people may find comfort and guidance in exploring past lives, it's important to approach the subject with an open mind and to consider one's own personal beliefs and experiences. Additionally, it's important to remember that ultimately, it's an individual's actions in the present that shape their future.

The impact of past lives on relationships and life paths is a complex and nuanced topic that is rooted in the belief that unresolved issues and experiences from past lives can carry over and influence current relationships and life paths. While some people may find comfort and guidance in exploring past lives, it's important to approach the subject with an open mind and to consider one's own personal beliefs and experiences. Additionally, it's important to remember that ultimately, it's an individual's actions in the present that shape their future and the idea of past lives is not universally accepted and not scientifically proven.

Another way that past lives can impact relationships is through the idea of karmic relationships. According to this belief, certain individuals are brought together in this life to work through unresolved issues and karma from past lives. These relationships can be intense and challenging, as past life issues and karma can surface and create tension and conflict. However, they can also be incredibly transformative, as individuals can work through these issues and achieve greater understanding and growth in the relationship.

Additionally, past lives can also impact relationships through the idea of reincarnation. According to this belief, the soul or consciousness of an individual is reborn into a new body after death, which allows them to continue their journey of spiritual growth and development. This can include continuing relationships with the same souls from past lives, which can manifest as feeling a deep connection or familiarity with certain individuals in this life.

Furthermore, past lives can also impact an individual's life path by influencing their personal and spiritual growth. Some people believe that unresolved issues and experiences from past lives can hold them back from reaching their full potential in this life, and that by understanding and resolving these issues, they can achieve greater spiritual growth and fulfillment.

The idea of past lives and its impact on current relationships and life paths can be used in a therapeutic context. Some therapists and practitioners use past life regression therapy to help individuals explore and understand their past lives and the unresolved issues and karma that may be impacting their current relationships and life paths. However, it's important to approach these therapies with caution, as there is currently no scientific evidence to support their effectiveness and it's important for a therapist or practitioner to consider the possibility of confabulation, which means that the person is creating a story that is not true but seems real to them.

It's also important to consider that the idea of past lives and its impact on current relationships and life paths can be a personal and emotional topic. It's essential to approach the subject with sensitivity and respect, and to remember that what may be true for one person may not be true for another. Each individual's past life beliefs and experiences should be considered on a case by case basis.

Another point to consider is that exploring past lives and the connection with karma may not be necessary for some individuals to understand and improve their current relationships and life paths, as the current life and its experiences are enough to work through and improve the situation.

The impact of past lives on relationships and life paths is a complex and nuanced topic that is rooted in the belief that unresolved issues and experiences from past lives can carry over and influence current relationships and life paths. While some people may find comfort and guidance in exploring past lives, it's important to approach the subject with an open mind and to consider one's own personal beliefs and experiences.

Additionally, it's important to remember that ultimately, it's an individual's actions in the present that shape their future and the idea of past lives and its impact is not universally accepted and not scientifically proven. It's also important to approach the subject with sensitivity and respect, and to remember that what may be true for one person may not be true for another. Additionally, it's important to remember that exploring past lives and understanding the connection with karma may not be necessary for some individuals to improve their current relationships and life paths. It's essential to approach the subject with a holistic perspective and to consider the individual's overall well-being, rather than solely focusing on past lives.

It's also worth noting that while the idea of past lives and its impact on current relationships and life paths can be a powerful tool for personal growth and self-discovery, it's important to remember that it should not be used as a crutch for avoiding responsibility for one's current actions and choices. It's important to take ownership of one's current life and to use the understanding of past lives and karma as a tool for personal growth, rather than an excuse for avoiding personal responsibility.

The impact of past lives on relationships and life paths is a complex and nuanced topic that is rooted in the belief that unresolved issues and experiences from past lives can carry over and influence current relationships and life paths. While some people may find comfort and guidance in exploring past lives, it's important to approach the subject with an open mind, considering one's personal beliefs and experiences, but also being cautious about accepting it as a fact without any scientific evidence. Additionally, it's important to remember that ultimately, it's an individual's actions in the present that shape their future, and that exploring past lives and understanding the connection with karma may not be necessary for some individuals to improve their current relationships and life paths.

Another way that past lives can influence the current life is through the concept of unfinished business. According to this belief, unresolved issues or unfinished tasks from a past life can carry over into the current life, manifesting as recurring patterns, unresolved emotions, or unfulfilled desires. By identifying and resolving these issues, individuals can break free from these patterns and find a sense of peace and fulfillment in their current life. Past life beliefs can also provide explanations for certain aspects of one's current life, such as unexplained phobias or aversions, or a sense of familiarity with certain people or places. Some people believe that these experiences can be linked to past lives.

For example, an individual may have a phobia of heights and believe that this fear is rooted in a past life where they were harmed or killed in a fall. On the other hand, it's important to note that past life memories can be influenced by imagination, fantasy or suggestion during hypnosis, it's important for a therapist or practitioner to approach the subject with caution, and to consider the possibility of confabulation, which means that the person is creating a story that is not true but seems real to them.

Overall, the concept of past lives can be a complex and nuanced topic, and different people may have different beliefs and understandings of how past lives impact the current life. Some people may find comfort and guidance in exploring past lives, while others may not find it relevant to their life or spiritual beliefs. It's important for individuals to approach the subject with an open mind and to consider their own personal beliefs and experiences.

It's important to note that the concept of past lives is not a widely accepted or scientifically proven theory. While some people may find comfort and guidance in exploring past lives, there is currently no scientific evidence to support the existence of past lives or the impact that they may have on the current life.

Furthermore, it's worth noting that the idea of past lives can be used to explain away personal responsibility, and can be used as an excuse for not taking action to change one's current life. While exploring past lives can be an interesting and enlightening experience, it's important for individuals to keep in mind that ultimately, it's their actions in the present that shape their future.

Additionally, it's important to remember that past life beliefs and experiences can be highly personal and emotional. It's important to approach the subject with sensitivity and respect, and to remember that what may be true for one person may not be true for another. Each individual's past life beliefs and experiences should be considered on a case by case basis.

The concept of past lives is a complex and nuanced topic that can evoke different reactions and reactions. It's important to approach the subject with an open mind and to consider one's own personal beliefs and experiences. It's also important to remember that past life beliefs and experiences are not widely accepted or scientifically proven, and it's important to keep in mind that ultimately, it's one's actions in the present that shape their future.

The connection between past lives and karma is a complex and nuanced topic that is rooted in ancient spiritual beliefs and practices. Karma is a central concept in many Eastern religions, including Hinduism, Buddhism, and Jainism, and it refers to the idea that one's actions in this life will have consequences in future lives. According to this belief, good actions will lead to positive outcomes, while negative actions will lead to negative consequences.

In many Eastern spiritual traditions, the concept of past lives is closely tied to the idea of karma. According to these beliefs, the actions and experiences of one's past lives can influence the present and future lives through the accumulation of karma. The idea is that the karma from past lives can manifest in the form of physical, emotional, and mental patterns, experiences, and circumstances in the current life.

For example, an individual who has accumulated negative karma from past lives may experience negative patterns, such as chronic health issues or financial difficulties in their current life. On the other hand, an individual who has accumulated positive karma may experience positive patterns, such as good health and financial prosperity.

Some spiritual practitioners believe that by understanding the connections between past lives and karma, they can gain insight into the patterns and experiences of their current life, and make conscious choices to change negative patterns and experiences. They believe that by resolving the unresolved issues of the past lives, one can break free from negative patterns and experiences and achieve a sense of peace and fulfillment in the present.

The connection between past lives and karma is not a widely accepted or scientifically proven theory. While some people may find comfort and guidance in exploring the connections between past lives and karma, it's important to remember that there is currently no scientific evidence to support the existence of past lives or the impact that they may have on the current life.

Additionally, it's important to approach the subject of past lives and karma with caution, as the memories can be influenced by imagination, fantasy or suggestion during hypnosis and it's important for a therapist or practitioner to consider the possibility of confabulation, which means that the person is creating a story that is not true but seems real to them.

The Deja Vu Enigma

The connection between past lives and karma is rooted in ancient spiritual beliefs and practices. It's important to approach the subject with an open mind and to consider one's own personal beliefs and experiences. However, it's also important to remember that the connection between past lives and karma is not widely accepted or scientifically proven, and it's important to keep in mind that ultimately, it's one's actions in the present that shape their future.

Another aspect of the connection between past lives and karma is the idea of reincarnation. According to this belief, the soul or consciousness of an individual is reborn into a new body after death. This allows the individual to continue their journey of spiritual growth and development, and to work through any unresolved issues or karma from past lives.

The concept of reincarnation also suggests that people may have lived multiple lives, and that their current life is just one of many. This belief can provide a sense of continuity and purpose to an individual's life, and can help them understand the connections between their current experiences and their past lives.

In some spiritual traditions, the concept of past lives and karma is closely tied to the idea of spiritual evolution and the attainment of enlightenment. According to these beliefs, the soul is on a journey of spiritual growth and development, and the experiences of past lives and the accumulation of karma are all part of this journey.

The idea is that by understanding and resolving the unresolved issues and karma from past lives, an individual can progress along their spiritual journey and ultimately reach a state of enlightenment.

It's important to note that the concept of past lives and karma is not universally accepted and different people may have different beliefs and understandings of how past lives impact the current life. Some people may find comfort and guidance in exploring past lives, while others may not find it relevant to their life or spiritual beliefs.

It's also important to remember that the concept of past lives and karma is not universally accepted and it is not a widely accepted or scientifically proven theory. It's important to approach the subject with an open mind and to consider one's own personal beliefs and experiences. It's also important to keep in mind that ultimately, it's one's actions in the present that shape their future.

The connection between past lives and karma that is rooted in ancient spiritual beliefs and practices. It can provide a sense of continuity and purpose to an individual's life, and can help them understand the connections between their current experiences and their past lives. While some people may find comfort and guidance in exploring past lives, it's important to remember that the connection between past lives and karma is not universally accepted and not scientifically proven. It's important for individuals to approach the subject with an open mind and to consider their own personal beliefs and experiences.

The concept of past lives and karma can also be applied to understanding and resolving relationship issues. Some people believe that the unresolved issues and karma from past lives can manifest in the form of relationship patterns, such as attraction to certain types of people, or difficulty in maintaining healthy relationships. According to this belief, by understanding and resolving the unresolved issues and karma from past lives, an individual can break free from negative relationship patterns and attract healthier and more fulfilling relationships in the present.

Furthermore, the concept of past lives and karma can also be applied to understanding and resolving career and professional issues. Some people believe that unresolved issues and karma from past lives can manifest in the form of career and professional patterns, such as difficulty in achieving success or feeling unfulfilled in one's work. According to this belief, by understanding and resolving the unresolved issues and karma from past lives, an individual can break free from negative career and professional patterns and achieve greater success and fulfillment in their current profession.

It's also important to note that the concept of past lives and karma can be used in a therapeutic context. Some therapists and practitioners use past life regression therapy to help individuals explore and understand their past lives and the unresolved issues and karma that may be impacting their current life. However, it's important to approach these therapies with caution, as there is currently no scientific evidence to support their effectiveness and it's important for a therapist or practitioner to consider the possibility of confabulation, which means that the person is creating a story that is not true but seems real to them.

The connection between past lives and karma is complex and can be applied to understanding and resolving a wide range of issues, including physical, emotional, and mental patterns, relationship issues, career and professional issues. While some people may find comfort and guidance in exploring past lives and karma, it's important to remember that the connection between past lives and karma is not universally accepted and not scientifically proven. It's important for individuals to approach the subject with an open mind and to consider their own personal beliefs and experiences. And it's important for individuals to be cautious when engaging in past life regression therapy.

It's also important to consider the cultural context when discussing the connection between past lives and karma. In many Eastern cultures, the belief in past lives and karma is deeply ingrained in the cultural and spiritual practices. It is considered a fundamental concept that shapes the way individuals understand themselves and the world around them. In these cultures, the belief in past lives and karma is often intertwined with other spiritual concepts, such as the idea of spiritual evolution and the attainment of enlightenment.

On the other hand, in Western cultures, the belief in past lives and karma is not as widely accepted and is often considered a more alternative or fringe belief. However, in recent years, there has been a growing interest in Eastern spiritual practices and beliefs, including the concept of past lives and karma. This has led to an increasing number of Westerners exploring and incorporating these concepts into their personal beliefs and practices.

It's also important to note that the concept of past lives and karma can be a personal and emotional topic. It's essential to approach the subject with sensitivity and respect, and to remember that what may be true for one person may not be true for another. Each individual's past life beliefs and experiences should be considered on a case by case basis.

Additionally, it's crucial to remember that the connection between past lives and karma is not a universally accepted or scientifically proven theory. It's important to approach the subject with an open mind and to consider one's own personal beliefs and experiences, but also to be cautious about accepting it as a fact without any scientific evidence.

The connection between past lives and karma is rooted in ancient spiritual beliefs and practices. It's important to approach the subject with an open mind and to consider one's own personal beliefs and experiences, but also to be cautious about accepting it as a fact without any scientific evidence. It's also important to consider the cultural context and to approach the subject with sensitivity and respect, and to remember that what may be true for one person may not be true for another.

It's also worth mentioning that the connection between past lives and karma can be a powerful tool for personal growth and self-discovery. By exploring past lives and understanding the unresolved issues and karma that may be impacting their current life, individuals can gain insight into their own behavior patterns, emotions, and experiences. This can help them identify and overcome limiting beliefs, negative patterns, and unresolved issues, leading to greater self-awareness, personal growth, and inner peace.

Additionally, the concept of past lives and karma can provide a sense of meaning and purpose to an individual's life. By understanding the connections between their current experiences and their past lives, individuals can gain a deeper understanding of their personal journey and the role they play in the larger cosmic scheme. This can provide them with a sense of direction and purpose, and can help them navigate the challenges and opportunities of their current life.

The Deja Vu Enigma

It's also worth noting that there are different methods and techniques that can be used to explore past lives and understand the connection between past lives and karma. Some people may choose to use meditation, journaling, or visualization to access their past lives, while others may prefer to work with a trained therapist or practitioner who specializes in past life regression therapy. It's important to find a method or technique that resonates with one's personal beliefs and experiences.

The connection between past lives and karma is a complex topic that is rooted in ancient spiritual beliefs and practices. It can provide a sense of continuity, purpose and meaning to an individual's life, and can help them understand the connections between their current experiences and their past lives. By exploring past lives and understanding the unresolved issues and karma that may be impacting their current life, individuals can gain insight into their own behavior patterns, emotions, and experiences. However, it's important to remember that the connection between past lives and karma is not universally accepted and not scientifically proven. It's important to approach the subject with an open mind and to consider one's own personal beliefs and experiences, but also to be cautious about accepting it as a fact without any scientific evidence.

The impact of past lives on relationships and life paths is rooted in the belief that unresolved issues and experiences from past lives can carry over and influence current relationships and life paths. According to this belief, past lives can shape an individual's behavior patterns, emotions, and experiences in their current life, which can impact their relationships and life paths.

One way that past lives can impact relationships is through the concept of soulmates or twin flames. Some people believe that certain individuals are connected through past lives and that they are meant to meet and be in a relationship in this life. These relationships can be incredibly powerful and fulfilling, but they can also be challenging and difficult, as past life issues and karma can surface and create tension in the relationship.

Another way that past lives can impact relationships is through the concept of unfinished business. According to this belief, unresolved issues or unfinished tasks from a past life can carry over into the current life, manifesting as recurring patterns, unresolved emotions, or unfulfilled desires. These unresolved issues can create tension and conflict in relationships, as individuals may struggle to understand and resolve the underlying issues.

Past lives can also impact life paths by influencing an individual's career and professional choices. Some people believe that unresolved issues or experiences from past lives can manifest as blocks or obstacles in an individual's career and professional life. By understanding and resolving these issues, individuals can break free from negative patterns and achieve greater success and fulfillment in their current profession.

The Deja Vu Enigma

The concept of past lives can also provide explanations for certain aspects of one's current life, such as unexplained phobias or aversions, or a sense of familiarity with certain people or places. Some people believe that these experiences can be linked to past lives. For example, an individual may have a phobia of heights and believe that this fear is rooted in a past life where they were harmed or killed in a fall.

It's important to note that the belief in past lives and the impact on current relationships and life paths is not universally accepted and not scientifically proven. While some people may find comfort and guidance in exploring past lives, it's important to approach the subject with an open mind and to consider one's own personal beliefs and experiences. Additionally, it's important to remember that ultimately, it's an individual's actions in the present that shape their future.

The impact of past lives on relationships and life paths is rooted in the belief that unresolved issues and experiences from past lives can carry over and influence current relationships and life paths. While some people may find comfort and guidance in exploring past lives, it's important to approach the subject with an open mind and to consider one's own personal beliefs and experiences. Additionally, it's important to remember that ultimately, it's an individual's actions in the present that shape their future and the idea of past lives is not universally accepted and not scientifically proven.

Another way that past lives can impact relationships is through the idea of karmic relationships. According to this belief, certain individuals are brought together in this life to work through unresolved issues and karma from past lives. These relationships can be intense and challenging, as past life issues and karma can surface and create tension and conflict. However, they can also be incredibly transformative, as individuals can work through these issues and achieve greater understanding and growth in the relationship.

Additionally, past lives can also impact relationships through the idea of reincarnation. According to this belief, the soul or consciousness of an individual is reborn into a new body after death, which allows them to continue their journey of spiritual growth and development. This can include continuing relationships with the same souls from past lives, which can manifest as feeling a deep connection or familiarity with certain individuals in this life.

Furthermore, past lives can also impact an individual's life path by influencing their personal and spiritual growth. Some people believe that unresolved issues and experiences from past lives can hold them back from reaching their full potential in this life, and that by understanding and resolving these issues, they can achieve greater spiritual growth and fulfillment.

It's also worth noting that the idea of past lives and its impact on current relationships and life paths can be used in a therapeutic context.

The Deja Vu Enigma

Some therapists and practitioners use past life regression therapy to help individuals explore and understand their past lives and the unresolved issues and karma that may be impacting their current relationships and life paths. However, it's important to approach these therapies with caution, as there is currently no scientific evidence to support their effectiveness and it's important for a therapist or practitioner to consider the possibility of confabulation, which means that the person is creating a story that is not true but seems real to them.

It's also important to consider that the idea of past lives and its impact on current relationships and life paths can be a personal and emotional topic. It's essential to approach the subject with sensitivity and respect, and to remember that what may be true for one person may not be true for another. Each individual's past life beliefs and experiences should be considered on a case by case basis.

Another point to consider is that exploring past lives and the connection with karma may not be necessary for some individuals to understand and improve their current relationships and life paths, as the current life and its experiences are enough to work through and improve the situation.

The impact of past lives on relationships and life paths is rooted in the belief that unresolved issues and experiences from past lives can carry over and influence current relationships and life paths. While some people may find comfort and guidance in exploring past lives, it's important to approach the subject with an open mind and to consider one's own personal beliefs and experiences.

Additionally, it's important to remember that ultimately, it's an individual's actions in the present that shape their future and the idea of past lives and its impact is not universally accepted and not scientifically proven. It's also important to approach the subject with sensitivity and respect, and to remember that what may be true for one person may not be true for another. Additionally, it's important to remember that exploring past lives and understanding the connection with karma may not be necessary for some individuals to improve their current relationships and life paths. It's essential to approach the subject with a holistic perspective and to consider the individual's overall well-being, rather than solely focusing on past lives.

It's also worth noting that while the idea of past lives and its impact on current relationships and life paths can be a powerful tool for personal growth and self-discovery, it's important to remember that it should not be used as a crutch for avoiding responsibility for one's current actions and choices. It's important to take ownership of one's current life and to use the understanding of past lives and karma as a tool for personal growth, rather than an excuse for avoiding personal responsibility.

The Deja Vu Enigma

"Uncovering the Truth About Past Lives and Reincarnation."

Chapter 9

Healing Past Life Trauma and Negative Patterns

Past life trauma and negative patterns can manifest in various ways in our current lives, such as phobias, recurring relationship patterns, or physical ailments. The belief in past lives is not scientifically proven, but many individuals have found healing through past life regression therapy and other techniques that focus on resolving past life experiences.

One popular technique for healing past life trauma is past life regression therapy. This method involves inducing a state of deep relaxation, often through hypnosis, and guiding the individual back to a past life experience that may be causing current issues. The therapist will work with the individual to process and release any negative emotions or traumas connected to the past life experience. The goal is to bring a deeper understanding and acceptance of the past, leading to healing and a release of negative patterns in the present.

Another technique is the use of visualization and affirmations. This method involves creating a positive mental image of the desired outcome and repeating affirmations, such as "I release all past life trauma", to reprogram the mind and manifest positive changes in the present.

Other alternative therapies like energy healing, such as Reiki, can also be used to clear past life trauma and negative patterns. Practitioners work to balance the energy in the body and release any blocked energy that may be connected to past lives.

It's important to note that healing past life trauma and negative patterns can be a process and may require multiple sessions with a therapist or practitioner. It's also important to have a support system, whether it be friends, family, or a therapist, and to take care of oneself during the healing process.

It's also important to mention that past life regression therapy is not scientifically proven and some experts in the field of psychology raise questions about its validity and effectiveness. Also, some people might find it difficult to distinguish between past life memories and imagination, it is important to keep an open mind and approach it with a healthy dose of skepticism.

Overall, while the belief in past lives is not scientifically proven, many individuals have found healing through past life regression therapy and other techniques that focus on resolving past life experiences. It's important to work with a qualified therapist or practitioner and to approach the process with an open mind.

Another technique for healing past life trauma is the use of shamanic practices. This approach draws on ancient spiritual traditions, typically those of indigenous cultures, to connect with the spiritual realm and access past lives. This can involve the use of ritual, ceremonial practices, and the guidance of a trained shaman or practitioner. The goal is to retrieve lost soul parts, retrieve power, and gain insight and healing from the past life experience.

Some people also use meditation, which can be a powerful tool to access past lives. With regular practice, individuals can learn to quiet the mind and enter into a meditative state in which they can access past lives, retrieve lost soul parts, and gain insight and healing.

It is also important to address any physical symptoms that may be connected to past life trauma, such as chronic pain or illnesses. Many holistic practitioners believe that physical symptoms can be connected to past lives and that addressing these symptoms is an important aspect of healing.

It's also important to have a good understanding of the concept of karma, which is the belief that the actions and choices in past lives affect the present and future. By understanding and accepting the karmic lessons and resolving past traumas, individuals can release negative patterns and create positive change in their present lives.

Healing past life trauma and negative patterns can be a powerful process for individuals looking to gain insight and release negative patterns in their current lives. Techniques such as past life regression therapy, visualization, affirmations, energy healing, shamanic practices, meditation and addressing physical symptoms can be helpful in this process. It's important to work with a qualified therapist or practitioner and to approach the process with an open mind. It's also important to keep in mind that healing past life trauma and negative patterns is not scientifically proven and people should approach it with a healthy dose of skepticism.

Chapter 10

The Link between Past Lives and Spiritual Growth and Enlightenment

The belief in past lives is not scientifically proven, but many individuals have found that understanding and resolving past life experiences can have a profound impact on spiritual growth and enlightenment.

One way in which past lives can contribute to spiritual growth is by helping individuals to understand and release negative patterns that may be holding them back in their current lives. By gaining insight into past lives and resolving past traumas, individuals can release negative patterns and create positive change in their present lives. This can lead to a greater sense of self-awareness and personal power, which are key elements of spiritual growth.

Another way in which past lives can contribute to spiritual growth is by helping individuals to understand and accept the concept of karma, which is the belief that the actions and choices in past lives affect the present and future. By understanding and accepting karmic lessons, individuals can release negative patterns, create positive change and understand the purpose of their current life.

Past lives can also provide valuable insights into the nature of the soul and the continuity of consciousness. Understanding that the soul exists beyond the physical body and that consciousness continues after death, can help individuals to transcend fear of death and develop a deeper understanding of the nature of reality, which is important for spiritual growth and enlightenment.

Furthermore, past lives can also provide individuals with a deeper understanding of their purpose and the nature of their soul's journey. Through understanding past lives, individuals can gain insight into their unique talents, abilities, and lessons to be learned in this lifetime, which can help them to fulfill their purpose and live a more meaningful life.

It's important to note that past lives are not a requirement for spiritual growth or enlightenment, but can be a valuable tool for individuals seeking to gain insight and understanding. It's also important to keep in mind that past lives are not scientifically proven and people should approach it with a healthy dose of skepticism.

The Deja Vu Enigma

Overall, understanding and resolving past life experiences can be a powerful tool for spiritual growth and enlightenment. By gaining insight into past lives, individuals can release negative patterns, create positive change, understand the concept of karma, transcend the fear of death and understand the purpose of their current life. However, it's important to approach this topic with an open mind and skepticism, and it's not a requirement for spiritual growth and enlightenment.

Additionally, exploring past lives can also help individuals to understand their relationships and connections with others in their present life. It's believed that we often encounter the same souls in different lifetimes, and understanding these past connections can provide insight into why certain relationships feel familiar or why we may have a strong attraction or aversion to certain individuals.

Furthermore, exploring past lives can also help to alleviate certain phobias or fears that may have no apparent cause in this lifetime. It's believed that these fears may be rooted in traumatic experiences from past lives and understanding and resolving these past experiences can help to alleviate these fears.

It's also important to note that exploring past lives should be done with guidance, whether it be through a trained therapist or practitioner, or through self-exploration techniques such as meditation or past life regression.

These methods can help individuals to safely access and understand past life experiences, while avoiding the potential negative effects of unguided exploration.

While the belief in past lives is not scientifically proven, many individuals have found that understanding and resolving past life experiences can have a profound impact on spiritual growth and enlightenment. It can help individuals to release negative patterns, create positive change, understand the concept of karma, transcend the fear of death, understand the purpose of their current life and also help in understanding relationships and connections with others. However, it's important to approach this topic with an open mind and skepticism and always seek guidance when exploring past lives.

Another aspect of exploring past lives is the potential for personal healing. Many individuals may have unresolved traumas or emotional pain from past experiences that are carried over into their present lives. By understanding and resolving these past experiences, individuals can begin to heal and release these negative patterns and emotions. This can lead to a greater sense of inner peace and well-being, which is essential for overall spiritual growth and enlightenment.

Additionally, exploring past lives can also help individuals to gain a deeper understanding of the interconnectedness of all things. The belief in past lives suggests that everything is connected and that our actions in one life can have an impact on future lives. This understanding can lead to a greater sense of compassion and empathy for others, as well as a greater sense of responsibility for our actions. This can help to foster a greater sense of connection and unity with others, which is a key aspect of spiritual growth and enlightenment.

In summary, exploring past lives can be a valuable tool for personal healing, understanding the interconnectedness of all things and fostering a greater sense of compassion and empathy for others. However, it's important to approach this topic with an open mind and skepticism and seek guidance when exploring past lives. Additionally, it's important to note that past lives are not a requirement for spiritual growth and enlightenment, but they can provide valuable insights and understanding that can aid in the spiritual growth process.

Another benefit of exploring past lives is the potential for spiritual awakening. Many individuals may have a feeling of something missing or unfulfilled in their current lives. By exploring past lives, individuals can gain a deeper understanding of their soul's journey and purpose. This can lead to a greater sense of self-awareness and a sense of fulfillment in their current lives.

Additionally, exploring past lives can also help individuals to better understand the concept of reincarnation and the cyclical nature of life. By understanding that we have the opportunity to experience multiple lives, individuals can develop a greater sense of hope and optimism for their current lives. This can lead to a greater sense of purpose and motivation to make the most of the current life.

Furthermore, exploring past lives can also help individuals to overcome limiting beliefs and patterns. Many individuals may have limiting beliefs that hold them back in their current lives. By understanding the origins of these beliefs in past lives, individuals can gain the perspective and understanding needed to release them and move forward in their current lives.

It's also important to note that exploring past lives should be done with a non-judgmental attitude. Many individuals may have past lives that they may perceive as negative or shameful. It's important to remember that these past lives are simply experiences and that they do not define who we are as individuals. By exploring past lives with a non-judgmental attitude, individuals can gain valuable insights and understanding without feeling ashamed or guilty about their past experiences.

Exploring past lives can provide many benefits for spiritual growth and enlightenment such as personal healing, understanding the interconnectedness of all things, fostering a greater sense of compassion and empathy for others, spiritual awakening, understanding the concept of reincarnation, overcoming limiting beliefs and patterns, and should be done with a non-judgmental attitude. It's important to approach this topic with an open mind and skepticism and seek guidance when exploring past lives. Additionally, it's important to remember that past lives are not a requirement for spiritual growth and enlightenment, but they can provide valuable insights and understanding that can aid in the spiritual growth process.

The Deja Vu Enigma

"Uncovering the Truth About Past Lives and Reincarnation."

Chapter 11

Conclusion: Uncovering the Truth about Past Lives and the Deja Vu Enigma.

The belief in past lives is a topic that has captivated the imagination of many for centuries. The idea that we have lived before and will live again in future lives is a concept that is central to many spiritual and religious beliefs. However, the topic of past lives remains shrouded in mystery and is not scientifically proven. Despite this, many individuals have found that understanding and resolving past life experiences can have a profound impact on spiritual growth and enlightenment.

One of the most intriguing aspects of past lives is the phenomenon of deja vu, which is the feeling of having already experienced a particular situation or event. Many individuals have reported experiencing deja vu and often attribute it to a past life experience. However, the scientific explanation for deja vu is not entirely clear. Some experts suggest that it may be related to the functioning of the brain and memory, while others propose that it may be a manifestation of past life experiences.

Regardless of the scientific explanation, many individuals have found that understanding and resolving past life experiences can have a positive impact on their current lives. One way in which past lives can contribute to spiritual growth is by helping individuals to understand and release negative patterns that may be holding them back in their current lives. By gaining insight into past lives and resolving past traumas, individuals can release negative patterns and create positive change in their present lives. This can lead to a greater sense of self-awareness and personal power, which are key elements of spiritual growth.

Another way in which past lives can contribute to spiritual growth is by helping individuals to understand and accept the concept of karma, which is the belief that the actions and choices in past lives affect the present and future. By understanding and accepting karmic lessons, individuals can release negative patterns, create positive change and understand the purpose of their current life.

Past lives can also provide valuable insights into the nature of the soul and the continuity of consciousness. Understanding that the soul exists beyond the physical body and that consciousness continues after death, can help individuals to transcend fear of death and develop a deeper understanding of the nature of reality, which is important for spiritual growth and enlightenment.

Furthermore, past lives can also provide individuals with a deeper understanding of their purpose and the nature of their soul's journey. Through understanding past lives, individuals can gain insight into their unique talents, abilities, and lessons to be learned in this lifetime, which can help them to fulfill their purpose and live a more meaningful life.

It's important to note that past lives are not a requirement for spiritual growth or enlightenment, but can be a valuable tool for individuals seeking to gain insight and understanding. It's also important to keep in mind that past lives are not scientifically proven and people should approach it with a healthy dose of skepticism.

The topic of past lives and the deja vu enigma remains shrouded in mystery. While the belief in past lives is not scientifically proven, many individuals have found that understanding and resolving past life experiences can have a profound impact on spiritual growth and enlightenment. It can help individuals to release negative patterns, create positive change, understand the concept of karma, transcend the fear of death, understand the purpose of their current life and also help in understanding relationships and connections with others. However, it's important to approach this topic with an open mind and skepticism and always seek guidance when exploring past lives.

Additionally, it is important to note that exploring past lives can be a personal and subjective experience. What may be meaningful and insightful for one individual may not hold the same value for another. It is important to approach exploring past lives with an open mind, and be willing to question and validate one's experiences. It's also important to remember that exploring past lives is not a substitute for addressing current life issues, but rather a way to gain perspective and understanding.

One way to gain insight into past lives is through the use of past life regression therapy, which is a method where an individual is guided through a meditative or hypnotic state to access memories of past lives. It's important to seek guidance from a trained therapist or practitioner when exploring past lives through regression therapy, as it can have potential negative effects when done unguided.

Another way to gain insight into past lives is through self-exploration techniques such as meditation, dream analysis, and journaling. These methods can be used to access and understand past life experiences in a safe and self-directed manner.

The topic of past lives and the deja vu enigma remains a source of intrigue and fascination for many. While the belief in past lives is not scientifically proven, many individuals have found that understanding and resolving past life experiences can have a profound impact on spiritual growth and enlightenment. It's important to approach this topic with an open mind and skepticism, and always seek guidance when exploring past lives. Additionally, exploring past lives can be a personal and subjective experience and should be approached with an open mind, and be willing to question and validate one's experiences and also not be a substitute for addressing current life issues but rather a way to gain perspective and understanding.

It's also important to consider cultural and societal influences when exploring past lives. Different cultures and societies have different beliefs and perspectives on past lives, and it's important to be aware of these influences when seeking to gain insight into past lives. For example, some cultures believe in reincarnation as an integral part of their spiritual or religious beliefs, while others may not. Additionally, some individuals may be influenced by popular cultural representations of past lives in books, movies, and other media, which can also shape their understanding of past lives.

Another important aspect to consider is the potential for false memories when exploring past lives. It's important to be aware of the potential for false memories to be created during past life regression therapy or self-exploration techniques, and to approach these experiences with a healthy dose of skepticism. It's also important to be mindful of the potential for manipulation or exploitation by untrained or unethical practitioners who may falsely claim to be able to access past lives.

It's also important to remember that exploring past lives should not be viewed as a panacea for all problems. While it can provide valuable insights and understanding, it is not a substitute for addressing current life issues such as mental or emotional health concerns, and should be used in conjunction with other forms of therapy or self-help methods.

In conclusion, exploring past lives can be a valuable tool for gaining insight and understanding into one's self, and can help in spiritual growth and enlightenment. However, it's important to approach this topic with an open mind and skepticism, and always seek guidance when exploring past lives. Additionally, it's important to consider cultural and societal influences, the potential for false memories, and not be viewed as a panacea for all problems. Past lives are not scientifically proven, but can provide a valuable tool for individuals seeking to gain insight and understanding, and should be approached with caution and a critical mindset.

Suggestions for Further Resources and Support

1.   Past Life Regression Therapy: Many people find that working with a trained past life regression therapist can be a powerful tool for uncovering past lives and understanding the impact they have on their current life.

2.   Books and websites on Past Lives and Reincarnation: There are many books and websites available that provide further information on the topic, such as "Many Lives, Many Masters" by Brian L. Weiss, "Journey of Souls" by Michael Newton, and "The Reincarnation Sensation" by C.T. Keng.

3.   Meditations and Guided Imagery: Guided meditations and imagery can help to access past life memories and gain a deeper understanding of the role that past lives play in your current life.

4.   Support groups: online or in-person groups of people with similar interests in past lives and reincarnation can provide a supportive community and opportunities to share experiences and insights.

5.   Energy Healing: Some people find that energy healing modalities like Reiki and ThetaHealing can help to clear past life traumas and negative patterns, and to gain a deeper understanding of past lives.

6.   Personal Journaling: Keeping a journal can be a powerful tool for

exploring and understanding past life memories and experiences.

7. Lastly, always remember that it is important to approach this topic with an open mind and to be discerning when it comes to the information you find online or from other sources.

References

1.   Reincarnation and Biology: A Contribution to the Etiology of Birthmarks and Birth Defects" by Ian Stevenson, published in the Journal of Scientific Exploration in 1997.

2.   "Children Who Remember Previous Lives: A Question of Reincarnation" by Jim B. Tucker, published in the Journal of Consciousness Studies in 2005.

3.   "Reincarnation: A Critical Examination" by Paul Edwards, published in Prometheus Books in 1996.

4.   "The Case for Reincarnation" by Eileen J. Garrett, published in the Journal of the American Society for Psychical Research in 1940.

5.   "Reincarnation: The Phoenix Fire Mystery" by Sylvia Cranston, published in Julian Press in 1984.

6.   "Near-Death Experiences, the Restitution of Life and Reincarnation" by Pim van Lommel, published in Journal of Near-Death Studies in 2001.

About The Author

Ton'te Fairfax, author of The Deja Vu Enigma: Uncovering the Truth About Past Lives and Reincarnation." is a highly accomplished and versatile individual. She is a writer, researcher, talk show host, movie director, entrepreneur, game show host, and stand-up comedian. Fairfax began her writing journey at the age of 11, and has since developed a passion for self-help, personal development, and the supernatural. She is a creative and curious thinker who has dedicated herself to The Deja Vu Enigma researching and understanding the supernatural world and its connection to daily life. Her areas of expertise include theology, metaphysics, the law of attraction, hypnosis, meditation, and self-healing.

Fairfax is a dedicated writer and researcher whose work is centered on promoting a positive outlook on life and encouraging individuals to embrace laughter and love. She is continually exploring new perspectives and practices, and her expertise has made her a highly sought-after speaker, comedian, and educator. Her writing style is both educational and informative, providing valuable knowledge and inspiration for readers. With an array of forthcoming books, she remains committed to sharing her insights and wisdom with the world.

FB: comedienne Tonte Fairfax
TWT: TonteFairfax@comediantonte

Website: www.wombsrealitycheck.com
Email: wombsbytonte@gmail.com
Email : Tontefairfax@gmail.com

Thank You

I extend my sincerest gratitude to all those who have purchased any of my books. Your support is greatly appreciated and I am truly grateful for your belief in my work. Your investment in my books is a testament to your commitment to self-improvement and growth, and it is a privilege to be a part of your journey. Thank you for choosing my books as a means of expanding your knowledge and perspectives, and I hope that they continue to provide value to you.

<u>Upcoming Books</u>

The I AM Affirmation Journal

A Daily Practice for Manifesting Your Dreams

Unlock the Power of Life Energy:

Transform Your Mind, Body, and Spirit

Breaking the Cycle:

A Married Man's Journey to Overcoming Addiction and
Saving His Marriage"